Rod McKuen's

Book of Days

and a Month of Sundays

This book belongs to

____

Diary of the Year

____

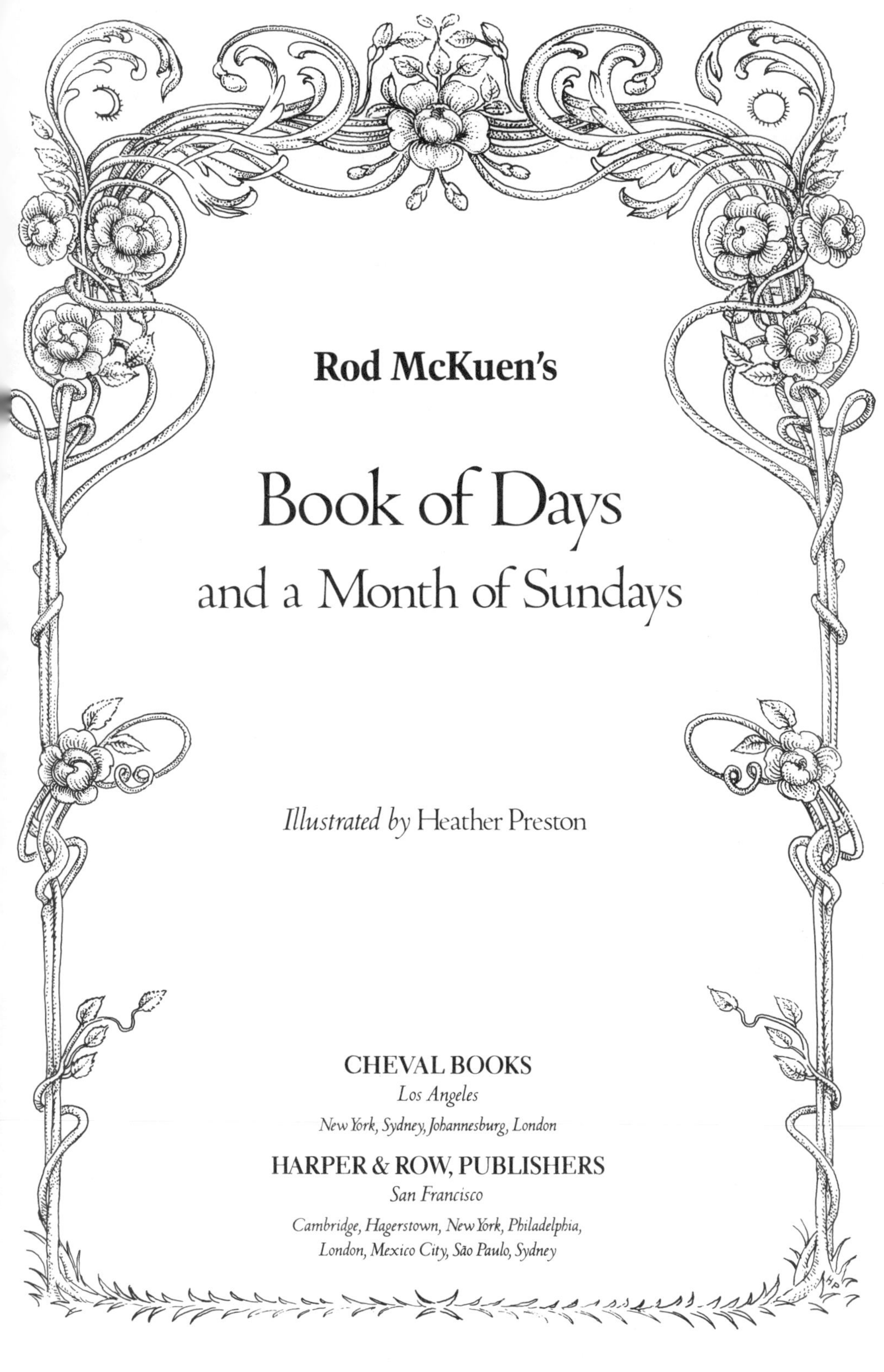

Rod McKuen's

Book of Days
and a Month of Sundays

Illustrated by Heather Preston

CHEVAL BOOKS
Los Angeles
New York, Sydney, Johannesburg, London
HARPER & ROW, PUBLISHERS
San Francisco
Cambridge, Hagerstown, New York, Philadelphia,
London, Mexico City, São Paulo, Sydney

 For information address Harper & Row, Publishers, Inc., 10 East 53rd Street, New York, NY 10022, or Montcalm Productions, 8440 Santa Monica Blvd., Hollywood, CA 90069.

FIRST EDITION: SEPTEMBER 1981

Designed by Marie Carluccio

Library of Congress Cataloging in Publication Data

McKuen, Rod.
Rod McKuen's Book of days.

1. Meditations. I. Title. II. Title: Book of days.
BV4811.M34 1981 242′.2 81-47421
ISBN 0-06-250569-6 AACR2

---

81 82 83 84 85 10 9 8 7 6 5 4 3 2 1

These thoughts have been
collected for my friends,
who know that friendship
means being a friend,
not having a friend,
loving rather than
being loved.

BY ROD McKUEN

BOOKS

Prose

Finding My Father
An Outstretched Hand
Rod McKuen's Book of Days

Poetry

And Autumn Came
Stanyan Street & Other Sorrows
Listen to the Warm
Lonesome Cities
In Someone's Shadow
Caught in the Quiet
Fields of Wonder
And to Each Season
Come to Me in Silence
Moment to Moment
Celebrations of the Heart
Beyond the Boardwalk
The Sea Around Me
Coming Close to the Earth
We Touch the Sky
The Power Bright and Shining
The Beautiful Strangers

Collected Poems

Twelve Years of Christmas
A Man Alone
With Love . . .
The Carols of Christmas
Seasons in the Sun
Alone
The Rod McKuen Omnibus*
Hand in Hand
Love's Been Good to Me
Looking for a Friend
Too Many Midnights

Music Collections

The McKuen/Sinatra Songbook
New Ballads
At Carnegie Hall
McKuen/Brel: Collaboration
28 Greatest Hits
Jean and Other Nice Things
McKuen Country
Through European Windows
Greatest Hits, Vol. I
Greatest Hits, Vol. II

*Available only in Great Britain

MAJOR FILM SCORES

The Prime of Miss Jean Brodie
A Boy Named Charlie Brown
Joanna
The Unknown War
Disney's Scandalous John
The Borrowers
Lisa Bright and Dark
Emily
Steinbeck's Travels with Charley

CLASSICAL MUSIC

Ballet

Americana, R.F.D.
Point/Counterpoint
Seven Elizabethan Dances
The Minotaur (Man to Himself)
Volga Song
Full Circle
The Plains of My Country
Dance Your Ass Off
The Man Who Tracked the Stars

Opera

The Black Eagle

Concertos

For Piano & Orchestra
For Cello & Orchestra
For Orchestra & Voice
For Guitar & Orchestra
#2 for Piano & Orchestra
For Four Harpsichords
Seascapes for Piano

Symphonies, Symphonic Suites, etc.

Symphony No. 1
Symphony No. 2
Ballad of Distances
The City
Symphony No. 3
Symphony No. 4
4 Quartets for Piano & Strings
4 Trios for Piano & Strings
Adagio for Harp & Strings
Rigadoon for Orchestra

To the Authors from the Author

(Assuming many of you will write in this book along with me)

Man has his seasons. His own times.
And while nature makes the colors change, the moons, the tides,
man is more accountable for change than he might know.

A *Book of Days* can be a diary, a collection of ideas, a series of dates to be remembered, a means of putting order into an otherwise orderless life, a storehouse of maxims (as well as "minimums"), a secret place to treasure private thoughts, or a book to help rekindle the heart or mind's memory.

I have chosen to make my first *Book of Days* all of the above. Instead of starting with January and following the calendar year—I don't know anyone who successfully keeps a diary that way—I began this book with my favorite season, autumn, and worked from there through winter, spring, and summer.

You will find no particular year set out in this book, because the memories go back as far as my capacity to remember; the years covered are many. Besides, if you plan to write in this book too, it's unfair to tell you where to begin or where to leave off.

There is space set out for every day of every month, but if you want to remember whether the third of April of some year fell on a Thursday or a Friday, you'll have to remember to write the year in for yourself.

For me, the best part of the book is the Month of Sundays near the end. Sunday is always a good day for me. For one thing, the telephone doesn't ring. Parts of the day can be given over to God and to leisure (sleeping late, reading the paper, playing with the animals).

Like everybody else, I have opinions on just about everything. Sometimes I keep them to myself; more often they wind up in my books, letters, interviews, and conversations. They change even while they are escaping. Collected here are opinions, a little philosophy, some truths I've learned, paragraphs that might be thought by some to be overly intimate, and ideas I felt like sharing. And there is plenty of room for your own ideas, memories, dates to remember, diary entries, and, right next to my thoughts, your arguments for or against.

Have fun. I did.

R. M.

Rod McKuen's

Book of Days
and a Month of Sundays

SOME THOUGHTS ON AUTUMN

If you're alone in autumn, you'll be alone all winter long.
And so security becomes not just the scepter or the wand
but the banner we hold high for confidence while we go
looking for safety that is real, sure security. For me
autumn is never a time of decay or age, but one of optimism,
knowing something, someone, waits. I am at one with nature
in the fall, and love and loyalty are as important to me
with new friends as they are with those collected down a lifetime.

Autumn

September

SEPTEMBER 10

September tenth . . . the year starts home.
Morning broke clear today
no fog . . . no rain
only a clear cold September morning.

It's autumn all right
you can feel it
with the taste of summer sweat still inside my mouth
my lungs breathe autumn.

The year goes back from where it came
like a battered kite being brought in
like a watch spring unwinding
like children to houses
when darkness comes.

Now night hovers
and madrigals begin again.

from *And Autumn Came*, 1954

September is the edge of hope, and sometimes it's the center. Travel through it carefully, but with ease. 1

I'm in a hurry; I have no time to hate. But I have all the hours in the seasons left to me to give to love. 2

Friendship is not a substitute for living, it is an amplification. 3

4

If you run the corridors and highways of the heart
for too long, you'll find it difficult to pause, let alone to stop.

5

The business of autumn is letting it lie where it falls.
The business of man is picking up himself and every member
of his family who falls or stumbles in the yellow leaves.

6

I have no quarrel with your lovers,
only admiration for their taste.

7

You cannot measure on a scale what love is worth,
though one small gesture sometimes tallies the amount
as surely as any seasoned teller could.

8

I want simplicity to be my password and my code for caring.
Too much time is lost in sorting out the real
from what we pass off as reality.

9

I measure success by the ones who come back.

10 By leaning on someone you love, you help to hold them up.

11 Wisdom lurks between the lines;
it's seldom verbalized or written down.

12 There are no dragons anymore—only windmills,
nothing left to slay except the clock that goes on stealing time.

He or she who hasn't stumbled
and been picked up by strangers or a friend
still trembles on the edge of life, awaiting entrance.

13

To anyone who hasn't loved, hating comes easy.

14

If we go to beds of boredom knowingly,
we deserve the ill attention we receive.

15

16 No need to know what's up or down, over or across the road—unless the road leads *out*.

---

17 As animals should not be caged so love cannot be legalized or legislated. It must be able to run free.

---

18 You must approach a decade as gingerly as you would a wolf. Both are up to little good. Agitating them will only make each bare its fangs a little sooner than expected.

If there is panic in my eyes, it's surrounded by curiosity.

19

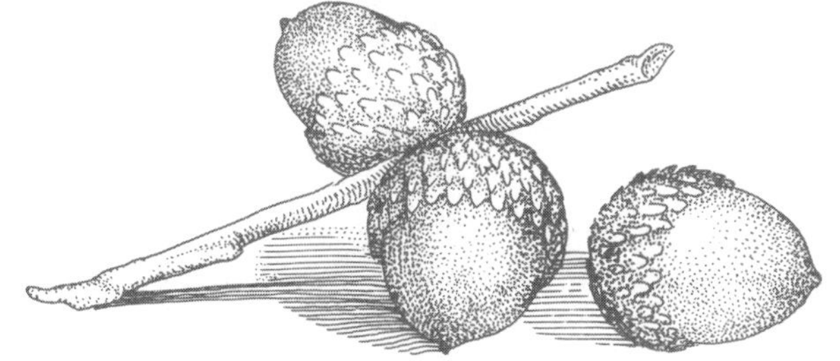

Enter into each relationship with trust.
Do not be easily convinced that something you want badly enough or believe in will not work.
Life works if you work at it.

20

The eyelids of the morning are of a different hue than those the sunset settles on us. So too is each woman and each man within the universal family different—
deserving of individual treatment.

21

22 Some pages in my diary are blotted or unused. Those must have been the happiest of times, for who can jot down happiness when it is happening?

23 The only thing we own without condition is experience.

24 I wish I had the addresses of all those friends
I knew and cared about twenty years ago.
I'd like to write each one and say that I'm okay—
and more importantly, that I still care.

To pretend you love someone is to cheat yourself as much as him. 25

I'm willing to change for you if necessary. But I want you only as you are. 26

Perhaps I've stayed within my rabbit hole too late, too long. I now almost enjoy that solitude I fought off for so long. 27

28

Lifetimes can be lived out in an hour
or loafed and wasted in a ten-year span.

29

To love somebody truly, it is not necessary
to be false to all other relationships.

30

Holidays mean the most when you're celebrating
what you've found yourself.

October

STATE BEACH

He turned
and moved to go into the water
she followed close behind.
The sun caught the color of her hair
and the bronze of his legs
and I caught them both
held them in my gaze
till they were out of sight
splashing in the sun
lost in the waves.

I think I have never been in love more than now
here on a native beach
watching other lovers
do familiar things and make familiar love.
I think I have never missed you more.

And as the last October sun
goes beyond the ocean to its resting place
and the umbrellas are folded
the rumpled pants and rumbled dresses
slipped over the wet bathing suits,
the sound of a Tokyo spring
echoes in my ears
I walk with you down dark streets
and the rain comes down like tears.

from *Stanyan Street & Other Sorrows*, 1966

1 October isn't just the month we wait for frost,
it is the time frost waits to tell *us* that it's time for change . . .
that change is coming whether we approve or not.

---

2 If we must judge, let us first
use the mirror on our own wall for practice.

---

3 So few promises are kept these days
that credibility must be stitched together from half-truths.
That should not cause despair, only diligence.

It is impossible to know a loved woman
who is not a beautiful woman.

4

A love that dominates is not love
but the most ill-gotten and ill-used form of possessiveness.

5

I wonder at teachers who demand instead of teach.

6

7

As bigots or as people who fail to take into account
other people's thoughts and needs and ideas,
we can never hope to be in God's good grace,
nor understand ourselves.

8

The leanest naked body is the work of God
and therefore a love object.

9

Security is an invitation to indolence.

Ideas have in common with the acorn the luxury of starting small and taking several lifetimes to become oaks. **10**

No man wants the hidden hand of anything to be his pilot.
Each of us believe ourselves to be the new Marco Polo
or Gulliver, or Chris Columbus. **11**

Encounters are the footsteps up and down the ladder
or through the littered alleyways of time.
As such, not to be taken lightly, or cherished
beyond their reality as food for the imagination's future. **12**

---

13 Each encounter that becomes a friendship turns into a lifeline. One can never have too many, only too many to take care of.

---

14 Men join clubs for the same reason they used to carry them—for security. But from what?

---

15 Passion seeps below the bedsprings to the slats and imperfections in the sagging floor. Truth hides back behind some door that no keys fit.

16

I love you enough to let you run
but far too much to let you fly.

17

Though I've been an islander most of my life,
I could sail around the world on *yes*,
if you'd once use it.

18

The heart has its reasons.

19

Love is the coming together of two ordinary people
in order to become one very extraordinary human being.

20

Before befriending butterflies
you have to meet with midnight moths.

21

Love is a four-letter word and should be used with discretion.

I've never known a cat who couldn't calm me down, just by slowly walking past my chair.

22

I can forgive anything but a lack of kindness.

23

To walk away from love is to turn your back on life.

24

25

Find a person who's wholly unselfish and you find one dead to dreaming.

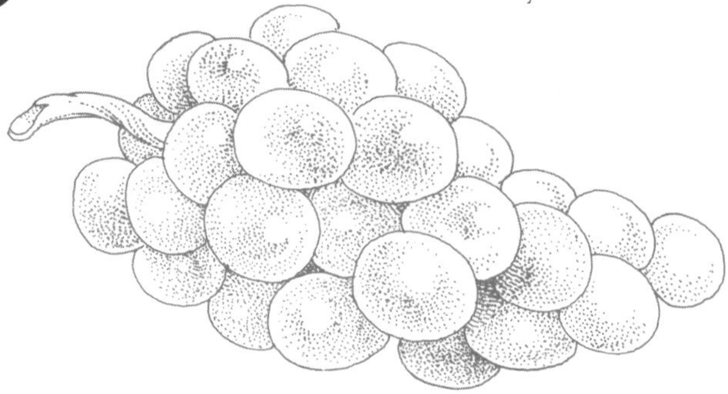

26

True love is totally open and committed to sharing not just the good times and the great moments together or apart, but the frustrations, loneliness, despair, and hurt generated by and exorcised by love.

27

I forgive my friends everything twice; then I begin to worry.

Whatever the arithmetic, the end of love is slow.

28

Don't compete. You're lesser than no man and none
are better. All creatures, beings, people are unalike.
How can you compete, win or lose a race,
with someone other than yourself? Being you
is hard enough, but someone other? Never.

29

Things do not change because of accident.
Man is not rearranged by man himself.
Man changes and is changed by something else.
We are altered by the alternatives we stumble on.

30

31

There are choices and choices that go wanting.
We wouldn't know of ghosts but for the haunting.

November

CATS

Cats have the best of it
I suppose they always have.
Curled up in autumn
back behind the stove,
swaggering through shrubbery
in the summer months
pirates seeking treasure
be it hapless mouse or moth.

When ready for some human contact
(usually as mealtime draws near)
they're friendlier to us than foxes
                    or the possum
but they do not extend lap dog submission.
A cuddle and a scratch behind the ear
                    is quite enough.

Cats, I reckon, have it all
admiration and an endless sleep
and company only when they want it.

from *I Never Met a Cat I Didn't Like*, 1982

1 For travelers, a block away, half a world away,
home is always over the next hill, always one more mile.

2 There will be times when many will want pieces of you,
but only offer up the whole.

3 We are chained only by ourselves. Our thoughts and actions are our jailers just as they can be the liberating angels that set us free to be ourselves.

Vote! It entitles you to bitch for the next four years. 4

Perspective comes when poles are far enough apart 5
to have horizons at both ends.

The sun is a movable target. Aim for something in life 6
a little more steady and less all-consuming.

7 Once I thought dreams were exceptions, not the rule.
But that isn't so—they are so plentiful that they ride by on air.
You've only to reach out and snatch one from the mist,
or from nowhere.

---

8 In making up a bed of love, be sure to leave the cushions loose.

---

9 Those who travel gentle in the world are seldom recognized
as gentlemen by others. It matters not, for gentleness
toward another human being is the thin line
between personal success and failure for each of us.

10

Few of us are ready to love anyone else—
until we learn to know and love ourselves.
That isn't easy, and it shouldn't be. It is difficult
both to love that much, and seemingly that little.

11

Those who are dead to dreaming live within a cloud
of their own making, and so their chance of entering
the stratosphere is scant.

12

Our country owes us nothing. We could not pay back what
she has given us already if we had two new lifetimes
left to attempt the job.

13 The day will come when we export more bread than bullets.
That day we'll know all there is to know of love.

---

14 Several men have proven that any man can grow up and become President—some of those same men have also shown us that not every man elected to the office is capable of *being* President.

---

15 If love hasn't given you wings, do not expect to fly.

To dream is to remain always open.

16

Wisdom is as slow to come as snow to melt.

17

Love, at best, is giving what you need to get.

18

19 Man is energy. The only energy we have is man.

---

20 Without some "think time,"
we relinquish our quest for knowledge to others
and are forced to accept their opinions as our own.

---

21 Special mysteries do not worry me
as much as what we do to one another
beneath the seemingly soft veneer of friendship.

22

Follow love and you need no other leader.

23

The few who say so much for all of us with knotted tongues
should die in poppy fields, old and withered, used up, done,
their last days spent as children once again.

24

In loving, nothing succeeds like excess.
Moderation is a mutual act and should be synchronized.

25

If I love my fellow man a little more today,
tomorrow I'll move more gently through *his* space.

26

We travel such a distance to stand still.

27

Taking the time to love is, most of all, caring enough
to not hold on too tightly and yet not run too loose.

Keep your finger on the country to monitor its pulse, but do not pass a mirror without looking at yourself. Remember that you are the country. **28**

Liking everything leaves little time for liking anything well. **29**

Cats know. They're as good as bank clerks at sensing loss or gain, better than the clairvoyant at seeing what's ahead. **30**

IN WINTER

In winter we return home again to whatever. Cold comfort. Warmth of friends. Strangeness. Death. We hibernate like bears. Seek private places to stay private in. Ward off colds. Christmas for the children. Loneliness for others.

There is a purity to winter. A calmness. The young are left alone because their elders dwell on loss and limits. This time excuses for reassessing involve the new year. Maybe the purity of winter has more to do with snow than stuff of stronger substance.

Finally mid-February brings the old and young together and a valentine is more than just a blood-red heart.

Winter

December

A MAN

To think that down through all these years
these stumbling, dancing decades
these hours given
to spend the way we wish,
that people of goodwill
in country, countryside,
                metropolis, and hamlet
come together / stay apart
but hold the selfsame ritual
as winter starts,
the celebration of an ancient birthday
deep in dark Decembers
too numerous to count.

He must have been extraordinary,
quite something,
to command the whole world pause
to celebrate His coming.

unpublished, 1958

I have known some winters 1
to allot a share of joy, not just in the carnival or on
the skating pond, but even in December's silence.

Without the cold for reference, 2
we wouldn't recognize the comfort of warmth.

Words have no more wisdom when it's time to say goodbye. 3

4 It seems to me the other parts contributing to calendars have too little quiet. Though winter can admittedly contain too much.

---

5 Where do they go,
the people who sail into our lives like green leaves
and disappear like snow?

---

6 Peace is a beautiful word . . . especially in practice.

Don't be too quick to question everything.
There are wild roses that have bloomed far into December
seemingly without reason. 7

We must continue to BELIEVE that many are the men of peace
who from time to time will set out to walk among us. 8

Sometimes, love follows where friendship leads,
but it doesn't always work the other way. 9

10 We gather strength through fidelity.

11 Sleeping's everything. It keeps the voluntary thought from forcing out the fantasy so that each of us can go on caring in safety.

12 I cannot be wounded by the stag, head down at charge—only by the words of those I love when they speak ill of me.

I am not convinced that truth alone can make us free,
but I believe it a beginning and a final resting place.

13

What I see convinces me there is a God.
What I cannot see confirms it.

14

A string untied needs tying up just as every empty space,
merely to prove its existence, needs walking through.

15

16 Who is not a love seeker when December comes?
Even children pray to Santa Claus.

17 The quest is not to seek out God, for He is everywhere. Rather, it is to learn more about Him. In so doing, we expand our capabilities and increase our knowledge of ourselves. Accepting God, then, is finally coming to accept ourselves.

18 Praying never hurt anybody, but wouldn't it be nice
to spend more time doing it for someone other than ourselves?

Love is an act of giving; giving is an act of love. **19**

How difficult it must be to want something so much, to be prepared for it, dressed up and ready — then in the end to be told chance and competition have been closed. But even in the face of "no," keep your eyes open. **20**

If you loved my face as much as you love Christmas, I'd be safe from year to year. **21**

22 So much pleasure comes from giving that it's almost stealing.

23 You get a lot more
if you're willing to settle for a lot less.

24 I wish you Christmas every time your eyes close. I pray that you will run with deer and soar with eagles, touching ground only long enough to find that one who'll love you every bit as much as I do and one you'll feel the same toward.

Though the gift be small and simple, if the wish is wide, just the simple gift of giving makes you warm inside. 25

Christmas is more than a celebration, it's a time of summing up. 26

Suicide is not a practical alternative to life, because tomorrow always carries in its very mystery a promise as well as a threat. That promise should not be denied. 27

---

28 Language has no ends and no beginnings
other than the coda each death makes and the paragraph
that starts with each new birth.

---

29 Beyond hello, before goodbye, there should be a string of words
or one long paragraph to make the ending easy.

---

30 If you love someone, tell them.

31

And now a toast: I wish you heady harvests every day of every year, no unsure hours or sleepless nights, and happiness enough to make the valleys of New England and the verdant hills of France forever green inside your heart.

January

PASSING THROUGH

We pass the signs
          the seasons
and the signposts now
at such a speed
that pausing to reflect
on what direction means
grows harder year by year
and yet your God and mine
daily holds His breath
expecting us to listen
and to care about each other.

Across the fields
beyond the highways
and each ocean,
I reach out to you
hoping I'll be welcomed
by another outstretched hand.

For each day
in the year just starting
and all those days in years ahead
I wish you love and reason
               in your life
and most of all
the feeling and reality
of our friendship.

from *The Beautiful Strangers*, 1981

Now comes another year, another chance to say thank you to old friends for staying close no matter what . . . 1

Everything is original when you find it out for yourself. 2

Mankind's greatest trouble is that we continue to forget that life is not a dress rehearsal. Each day acted out and done is gone forever. 3

4 The day you start insulting yourself, others begin to join you.

5 Daydreams are harder to realize as each day passes.
Few of us are wise enough to hold onto our visions.

6 Lie down with love, wake up with life.

Because pride seldom lets us beg forgiveness, we must content ourselves with dying a little every time a door is closed. 7

The most important thing I am is a guardian of dreams; the least important thing I am is me. 8

Love has no hidden highways, as hope hasn't any padlocked doors. 9

10

Extending your hand is extending yourself.

11

The surest way to love your enemy
is to recognize him as a future friend.

12

Smiles surprise people.

For me, no two or ten or two hundred make up a minority. Each of us is such, because each of us is different. **13**

What is finished should be finally done, not hung onto like a lifeline that will finally stretch and snap. **14**

To begin with, every page is blank, until a word, a smudge, a paragraph is set down upon it. I do not know how death will come to me, but I am resolved that, if I can, I will view the end as the writer does the blank page just in front of him, a beginning. **15**

16 Love is the bed you imagine others lie in, when you find yourself alone.

17 Equality means not only equal rights but equal responsibility to one's neighbor and one's self.

18 People really cry — a good thing to remember in taking love in stride, in taking love at all.

19

Because imagination sticks, gets caught, settles in
as we grow older, finally there is only one long, silent hour—
even if it lasts a day.

ASN'T UNTIL MID-SHOWER I REMEMBERED TODAY MAKE 27 YEARS OF
TINUOUS SOBRIETY. THANK YOU GOD for this miracle!

20

Death is not our final hour. We have God's promise on that.

R LONG NATIONAL NIGHTMARE IS OVER!" — WORDS OF
RALD R. FORD UPON ASSUMING THE PRESIDENCY IN 1974. THEY
ULD HAVE BEEN SAID WITH EQUAL FERVOR BY BARACK OBAMA
DAY!

21

When I die, I hope my heart and body will be
so scarred from love as to make an autopsy impossible.

22 The responsibility of preserving the nation for our sons and daughters cannot be passed over to officials or bureaucrats. To do so would be to give our hard-earned land away.

---

23 You wait for children to grow; you even hurry the process along with love. But still you're disappointed when they walk off on their own instead of being carried in your arms.

---

24 You cannot have the fatherhood of God without acknowledging the brotherhood and sisterhood of all human beings, the dignity, the beauty and the difference in all things He made.

Gossip hurts. It maims, it kills. Never pass along a half-truth,
a made-up fact, or a sentence you would say
to anyone but him or her you speak about. **25**

The only time I come out the winner
is when I race myself and pass the mark I've set before.
The trophies I collect are smiles. **26**

I am not afraid of what's upcoming or what has gone before
and if there's nothing left to know about or learn
I'll review the early lessons yet again. **27**

28 Be not a soothsayer, but a truth sayer, one who slays a lie as earnestly as a knight might skewer or carve a dragon.

---

29 War is a telescope whose other end is always fixed on darkness.

---

30 See all sides of everything before being sure of anything.

31

Silence is a better means of telegraphing thought than any Morse code yet made.

February

ANOTHER MONDAY, TWO MONTHS LATER

Now I have the time
to take you riding
        in the car
to lie with you
in private deserts
or eat with you
in public restaurants.

Now I have the time
for football all fall long
and to apologize
for little lies and big lies
told when there was no time
to explain the truth.

I am finished
with whatever tasks
kept me from walking
in the woods with you
                or leaping
in the Zanford sand.

I have so much time
that I can build for you
sand castles out of mortar.

Midweek picnics.
Minding my temper in traffic.
Washing your back
and cleaning out my closets.
Staying in bed with you
long past the rush hour
and the pangs of hunger
and listening to the story
                of your life
in deadly detail.
Whatever time it takes,
I have that time.

I'd hoped that I might
take you traveling
down the block
or to wherever.

I always wanted
to watch flowers open
all the way,
however long
the process took.

Now I have the time
to be bored
to be delivered
to be patient
to be understanding
to give you
all the time you need.

Now I have the time.

Where are you?

from *Moment to Moment*, 1972

1 I have known the most democratic community to consist of only two people dedicated to each other.

---

2 Years pass by within a single hour for those who feel uncared for.

---

3 I sometimes think rooms are the only comfortable places left. A room within a room would be the best place of all, an interior hiding place where solitude is the only company.

Loneliness is like guerrilla warfare. It undermines even the strong by small but frequent assaults. 4

The reader knows the rhyme.
The rhymer knows the reason. 5

Skating on your smile each night I know that I am safe.
And I am privileged beyond whatever God there is to watch with you 6
the man-made stars and those the master scatters out Himself.

7 Far-off unpeopled planets dart the heavens. If I can glide along your grin, the other worlds were truly made for only us.

8 Since the cure for selfishness is being willing to share, the remedy for certain kinds of loneliness is seeking out others, befriending them, or even asking for their help.

9 Live while the candle lives. Don't look ahead and wonder who, if anyone, will snuff it out.

10

Few angels have been heard to sing,
but many purr when stroked just so.

11

To hurt someone you love is difficult and takes no imagination.

12

Silence from enemy or friend speaks chapter
and speaks verse, especially when there is little to quarrel over
but the latest snowfall.

13

If love is elastic, don't stretch it.
Let it spread or snap back by itself.

14

It doesn't matter who you love or how you love,
but that you love.

15

Winter's contribution to the lilac root
will not be known for months, though tulip bulbs
may feel secure still frozen.

I believe, increasingly, that each of us is essentially alone. The trouble is, we're ill-equipped to live with it. **16**

The more attention we give the seed of loneliness, the more we allow it to grow. **17**

Good farmers don't harass the ground—until the ground is ready. **18**

19 One is usually not lonely for Schenectady or Paris or humanity, but for *someone*. He or she has left us, died or is missing, and has thus betrayed us. Loneliness is often self-induced, and being lonely could be considered selfish.

---

20 Silence often argues more than spit-out-speech.
Listeners hanging on expected words make up or envision
what they cannot, will not ever hear.

---

21 With love, it's either famine or a feast,
you've got to learn to smile at least and
store up pleasures for that rainy day love goes away.

If you stargaze long enough, you learn that no two fire balls or constellations are alike, and the star that shines the brightest is the one most different. Resolve, therefore, to be unique by being you. 22

How often we say *no* by saying nothing. 23

If you've a special talent, let it be the gift of discovering priorities that benefit the many. 24

25 How can there be an ending if nothing of importance has begun?

26 The best way to cure a cold is to go to bed with a good book or a friend who's read one.

27 Privacy is paramount to peace.

The calm that comes of one's own making is the most delicious of all treats. 28

Every year should have an extra day, just to throw away. 29

SPRING SONG

Long before the trees begin to bud, before the new grass starts to roll with the curvature of the hill and spread out evenly on the common, a certain uneasiness, a kind of insecurity arrives one morning or maybe just at dusk. It presents itself, moves in and settles in. Not unkind, not troublesome, this uncertainty is more an itch—a harbinger that finally scratched enough boils into the apple blossom.

The thrower of the seeds lets go his kernels in mid-March. The early April rain cooperates. Later on the lilac trees are all so heavy that their boughs bend low and nearly break. The prairie dog sits up and calls from mound to mound . . . a high pitched squeak that all his brothers answer. New pinafores for Sunday School. New patent leather shoes for Easter.

The May pole dance. Lost balloons begin to decorate the inside branches of trees. The Song of the Wandering Angus is lived out and sung. The plainest of us begin to feel beautiful again . . . and the fever deepens.

Spring

March

PLANTER'S MOON

The moment
that the planter's moon
started down across your back
and promised me a harvest
great and good,
I knew that I had crossed
a different kind of field,
greener than the ones
I'd trampled through before.
And if not safe
from all those hidden holes
and eyes lately
gathered in a crowd,
curious and hoping for the accident,
I knew it would be different.

I have kept my distance,
trying hard to keep the rules
and never violate the boundaries.
There are fences that I leapt
and some that I slid under,

even when I knew
I'd tear my pants.
Not equipped with hook and ladder
I scaled walls
and burst through barricades
                and balustrades
as sure as any second-story man,
as certain as a centipede
all systems working.

I kept my arms spread wide.
I teetered on a tightrope
            stretched between
your *sometimes* need for me
and tied securely
      by my *always* need for you.
Balancing,
        always balancing.
One foot before the other
down the rails and roads.

from *Fields of Wonder,* 1970

---

1 Spring speaks out to each of us, *kick the guts from your old dreams,* she says, and start a new and better dream. Don't waste your time merely thinking. Act. Do. Deliver.

---

2 My dog likes oranges, but he'll eat apples too. Don't bother me with your conventions and I'll not trouble you with mine.

---

3 Love should be a season of sunlight with only morning clouds for contrast . . . as endless as a life without illness, a tree that grows within a perfect climate during its young years so that it becomes stronger against the onslaught of the elements.

All people have lessons they can give us even in rejection. 4

There is no fresh air without love. 5

If truth exists, you have to seek it out—
but be patient, for nothing beautiful comes easy. 6

7

God's handiwork is as fleeting as a passing thought and as solid as stone.

8

Today I'd like to know the face of someone—anyone—I could blame my headache on.

9

Lift me up hard, but let me down easy.

Love unreturned is not necessarily unrewarded. **10**

Love carried to its highest point
is simple anticipation. So too is fear. **11**

No one of us can name, let alone free, those demons
that keep us from being the kind of men and women
we would like to be. **12**

13 Those who claim to have inferiority complexes may not have complexes at all.

14 The wolf who stops to measure the distance goes hungry.

15 How can we presume such easiness with each other and still remain so insecure?

From our birth we begin moving toward death. It may be that death upon this earth is only the shrugging off of a body grown weary, so that the soul can display itself in some better place.

16

Excess—great loneliness, great joy, great sorrow, great despair, great disappointment—is the mother of art. So it is that uncertainty often brings out the truth and the sureness in the things that we create.

17

Keep Spring waiting at your peril. She will not be held back even by an extra storm that wasn't in the Farmer's Almanac, the forecast in the morning paper, or the weather watcher's caution.

18

19 March not only to your own drummer but to your own syncopation, be you a band of many or one voice soloing, slicing through the silence, a single sound heard 'round the corner or 'round the world.

---

20 A cloud. No single eagle ever sat upon one, and guns while piercing some have never killed or wounded any. They multiply, divide, and multiply again. I've never seen a cloud destroyed and certain birds are buoyed by them.

---

21 The dandelion hasn't yet been known to make a choice between the pasture and the lawn, and love's as blind to rank and right as politicians are to pulsebeats.

Even when my memory has a favored day,
some prisoners refuse escape. 22

We'd salvage much, and save on doctor bills,
if we paused to read instructions. 23

I've counted moons, magnified them in a Moscow glass,
tripped on stars within the tropics,
and shared great armfuls of dim and distant light
in my own flatlands with no one but myself.
No storm can stop me now. 24

25 Truth is never absolute, as lies are seldom ever lies completely.
No one ever seems to notice or even try to take apart
that gray matter lurking in between the two.

---

26 I wish that I were plain enough to show you I'm but me,
or as fancy as I feel you think I should be.

---

27 Some people mistake patience for intellect.

The minute man walks into war
he starts into a tunnel with no end.

28

We should be nicer to each other. We're all we've got.

29

Age is only irrelevant to the young.

30

31

I glory seeing your reflection
coming back to me from other people's eyes.

April

APRIL IN THE EAST

Another field of April snow
The sun begins to slice
each knoll or tree
that blocks its view
until it strikes a lake
and falls from sight.
I mourn its going
as I mourn the now-gone day.

The birch so straight and strong
will not let the wildest storm
bend it to its knees.
One in every hundred hundred
is uprooted and falls down
and only then by accident
or God's design.

Birds and beasts and man
standing in a line
waiting for the thaw.
No sign as yet that April
will be anything but echoes
of December's past.
This winter's been the longest.

Let the snow make up
new rivers not yet named
or reinforce the old ones.
Let the green come sneaking
down the hills again
and climb the pines.
April, be not March or Monday.
Be yourself.

from *Coming Close to the Earth*, 1978

1

April is the answer to the unasked question:
Will things always be and stay the same?
For better and for worse—they will not.

2

Love is the most fun you can have without laughing.

3

Life quartered, life divided, is not life at all.

4

Some voice inaudible to man speaks to the month of April, and so we have pink blossoms everywhere.

5

We should set out on some journeys with only maps of our own choosing, no compass but the one we carry in our heads. If we should sail beyond the earth's edge, it will be our business only.

6

Love is another word for sharing. If you go out into and beyond the day with love in mind and heart, you are probably as close to life as you can ever hope to be.

---

7 Spring springs surprises faster than the wizard whizzes.

---

8 If time were not a trumpet always sounding out assembly and formations, I'd let work go whistling and send out obligations with the garbage.

---

9 Perhaps the closer we stay to earth, the better chance we'll have of being what each of us needs in someone else.

A sweet tooth doesn't always crave the richest cake.
Sometimes cookies and a glass of milk will do. **10**

Count twenty shades of green in April,
and you still miss half a hundred. **11**

We must become gardeners again to keep the country growing.
It is the farmer, not the fighter, who has the tools. **12**

13 If you don't know where you came from, you can't know where you're going.

14 I have known some men to wonder though I've never heard one ask what the enemy believes in.

15 If God could give His son for love, we can offer up our smiles.

Whether planting love or lima beans,
the good farmer goes carefully down his furrows.

16

Being without love too long makes us as ready as the rose . . .
to be caressed and then ruined by the rain.

17

Everything comes together in the spring.

18

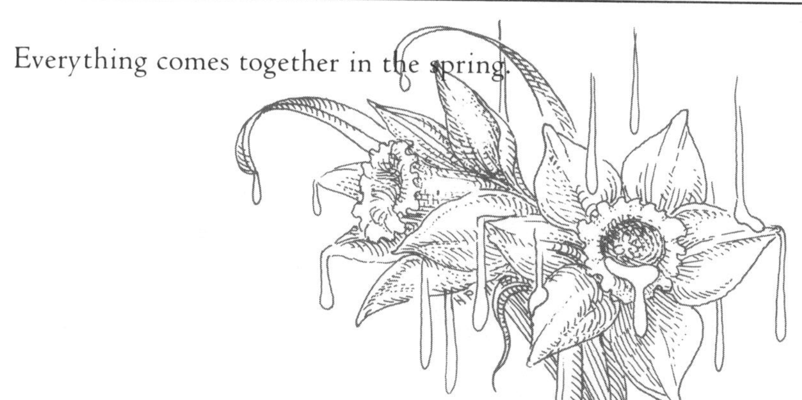

19 April won't apologize for children
seeking out irrigation ditches and mud puddles
in their search for the meanest place
to break in this year's brand-new Easter shoes.

20 Work is the four-letter word that made our country great.

21 Love must be the best life has to offer
for most of us are miserable without it.

22

April is the only time we need not ask God for miracles or transformation. They come unsolicited from everywhere, sent to us without prayer or lamentations.

23

No critic has a banner bright enough to carry me past the sunset, and no known or unknown legions unsheathe swords sharp enough to keep me silent. But I am willing to listen.

24

Reach down and grasp a handful of good ground—in doing so, you'll touch the arteries of angels.

25 I often think the furrows on your forehead
are wide enough to make a proper trench.
And then you grin.

26 Don't go yet, there's got to be some sea coast we've not seen.
Hold on to me and we'll go flying through the spring.

27 Friendship never wears a mask.
It removes the necessity for falseness and false faces.

Invest in your country by *investing in your friends.* 28

My mother gave me all her best rules for living.
I accept the blame for the mean and petty things
I've learned and sometimes practice. 29

The journey back is always longer than the forward run. 30

May

MAY 24/25

Spring will chase us
through the summer into fall
and find us beached upon some snowy shore
waiting for the spring to come again.

Then gingerly we'll go through jonquils
to seek out other summers.

Birthday to birthday
                    season to season,
every hour will be an anniversary
                              of the hour just past.

There are some forests
that I haven't known.
Some tree trunks
I have never wrapped my legs around
                    and climbed.
A million branches
I might have slid down
had I had the time.

Still
some leaves trembled in the wood
                                        and caught my ear.
Some twigs beneath the hooves of deer
                                          snapped and signaled *Spring*,
waking me from endless winter thoughts.

from *In Someone's Shadow*, 1969

Not reassurance but reason I need,
for spring's at the window slowing the day down. 1

I believe that, like the tide, my life has come
and gone in cycle after cycle. I've been dead
and resurrected many times. Who's to say it cannot
happen yet again? 2

What I want is not to be held accountable for what I said today,
or yesterday, so that my tomorrows can stay open.
Fat chance. 3

4 I presume that International Harvester can take its proper credit for bales of straw and wheat. But man must not forget who fostered love and fed it. He did.

---

5 The victory party isn't worth the having
if the celebrating's done in solitary.

---

6 Go forward, straight ahead. There are no limits on your life but those barricades you build yourself.

I've seen people drive into love without a learner's permit.
The result was usually an accident. 7

Love doesn't call for caution
as life does not depend on one man's way of living it. 8

The ocean has a lesson for our own lives and those we
take responsibility toward. *Push forward,* she keeps saying,
till your life is bare upon the shore, until you're naked to yourself and God. 9

10 How impressed we are with each other's nakedness.
But why?

11 I'd gladly go down in a whirlpool
if all day I had ridden on a friendly wave.

12 Each of us is earthbound, coming from the stars or wading to the shore. Sailing out, we must sail back—even if the voyage stops upon the ocean's bottom or beyond the universe.

There isn't anything I wouldn't do for you,
nor anything you wouldn't do for me.
So are we to spend our lives
doing nothing for each other?

13

Love is the only collateral for love.

14

To love, it is more important to learn the needs of others than to dwell upon your own.

15

16

I could be saved by hearing you say *no*
as surely as salvation lies on the velvet forehead of a *yes.*
Not knowing is a nod toward damnation.

17

Some oceans have been known to come again
to their mother country and wash ashore more brilliant treasures
than they took away.

18

The man who says *I told you so* is making an excuse
for not expressing his position clearly in the first place.

Friendship is an idea, not an invention, a pledge, not a promise, and (with any luck at all) a lifetime, not merely a season.

19

If the sea did not make me, at the very least it rubbed me,
rolled me out of darkness into light. For I have seen
my past and future on the whitecaps dancing out
beyond a thousand shorelines.

20

Love words roll from the tongue like ill advice.
Be careful.

21

22 The rhyme is in the rowing of the boat—straight ahead, not veering except to take on passengers. Steady hands circle sturdy paddles propelling us forever forward.

---

23 The supply of love will never exceed the demand, but it should.

---

24 The sea invents, we rearrange. The sea takes out a patent, we infringe. The sea holds all the copyrights to all the most important works, speaking truth that even time won't change. And still we steal from her.

Need can drive you down the darkest alley and leave you beached and bloody, waiting for the new encounter. 25

The sea eats up the men who love her most,
the way the killer queen must finally one day reject the troops
who fought for her on battlefields and rolled with her
in bedrooms. I am not afraid. 26

Love is an attitude, and one from which we should not stray far in our actions toward ourselves and others. 27

28 Something tugs at me, I've no doubt of that.
Something from the sea, whichever one I'm near.
When I stray too far from beachland, it calls me back.

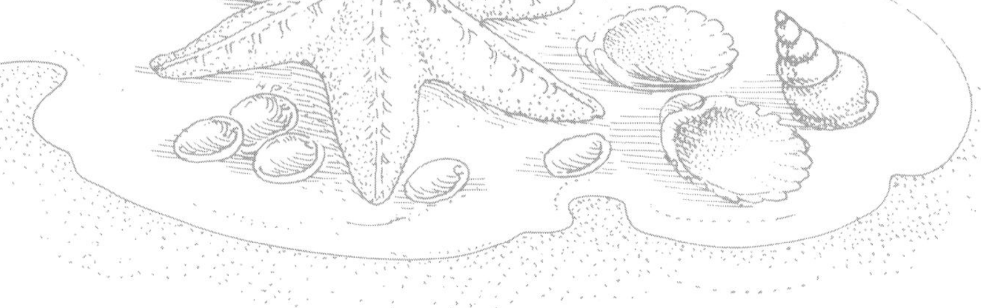

29 To deny the freedom of the will
is to make morality impossible.

30 To those who go ahead of us, we owe not just the ceremony
of a proper farewell speech, but a skeleton key
that opens all locks. Just in case.

31

If there is rest at all, we take our ease not on some hill of clouds or in the middle ocean. The notion that the earth is merely a departing place is hardly worth the time it takes to say so. Heaven and hell may fire our imagination, but surely ground and ground alone is home.

SUMMER SEQUENCE

The river cuts a gully every bit as deep within the
mind as the one it opens in the earth. Set your
troubles by, let the water carry them and you to that
wide, friendly sea beyond imagination. But all is
not imagined. The sun is real and everywhere.
Trials become truth. Goals turn round and round
until they spin into achievements.

And love? The firm, brown body running down the
beach—then gone. The soft, warm cheek that only
angels dare bend to touch. The round moon-belly
of a woman carrying the future just inside her skin.
The people old in years who commandeer a park bench,
and beyond them the lovers—always the lovers
discovering frontiers of gold.

Summer

June

ATLAS

Don't be afraid
to fall asleep with gypsies
or run with leopards.
As travelers or highwaymen
we should employ
whatever kind of wheels it takes
to make our lives
go smoothly down the road.

And if you love somebody
tell them.
Love's a better roadmap
for trucking down the years
than Rand McNally ever made.

from *With Love*, 1970

June is for juggling, for getting rid of spring
and moving into summertime. The beach is but
a backrest waiting to fold down into August. 1

Summer seldom comes at some appointed time.
Unbridled and unheralded, it jogs along toward September
in a forward, headlong run. 2

Every sparrow, once he's learned to serenade,
leaves the nest and ventures on his own to fly. 3

---

4 I sometimes fear that I'll explode, die, or disappear before I have a chance to tell the world how good I feel.

---

5 I have always been a man of the elements, feeling that the best ideas and the nearest thing to knowledge have to spring from the most real of all realities—the sea, the earth, the sky—rather than from history or philosophy books.

---

6 Let nothing pass between friends that lacks foundation in truth.

I always glance from right to left while passing down a new road. I'd hate to miss *the moment* when *it* comes along. 7

Love works best when we don't work at it. 8

Go easy. Take no one unaware.
Give each new friend, potential enemy, and lover time.
Never consciously return home with more than you have given. 9

10 I don't believe that I am happier while on the move, only that the need to go occurs and reoccurs.

11 Happiness costs pennies a day, sorrow millions.

12 I've no need to muzzle time. And, anyway, it's running at a pace I couldn't catch or stay abreast of even with the help of Mercury.

Being born amid the wealth and health of this prized nation, without the need to earn or win your share, is to be yet unborn. **13**

We lead small lives,
but they are made larger by what we do for one another. **14**

Loving for the sake of love
serves as much purpose as hating for the sake of hate. **15**

16 Everybody has the answers or they'll make them up for you. Just once I'd like to hear a brand-new question.

17 Fluorescent lights in public places were designed to challenge our good conceptions of ourselves.

18 If there still be those among you willing to commit to war, eager to do battle for the sake of battle, let them who sign the papers in the poolroom or the Pentagon be the first to shoulder arms and the only ones to feel the bullets.

Weight watchers may be looking at the wrong view. 19

I ford each river as I would the last and
take each lover as I would the final fatal one. 20

Each of us is quite alike in one way.
We wish only to be thought of as not alike. 21

22 Sometimes I think people were meant to be strangers.
Not to get to know one another, not to get close enough to
damage the heart made older by each new encounter.

---

23 Women are the managers, executives who
call the roll and keep things straight and honest—
with or without offices or titles.

---

24 I think perhaps that we are running, yes.
Always away, never toward.

The only ribbon I could safely stretch across my chest
is one to bind my heart and keep it from pounding
into nothingness when I feel loved.

25

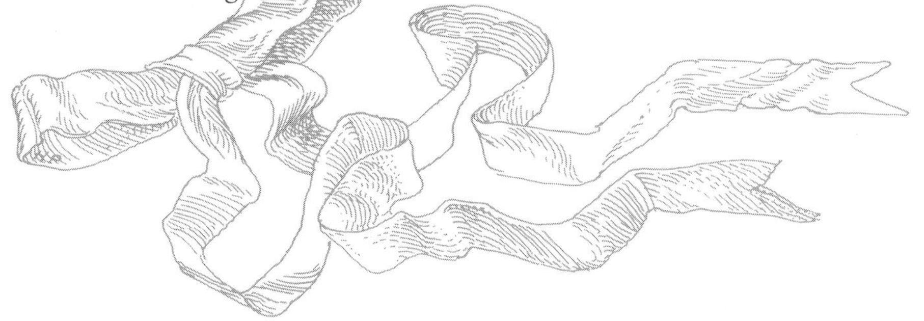

When the sand starts singing, no one will hear but us.

26

I am unprepared in thought or action
when a door I thought I helped to open
closes as I look the other way.

27

28

Freedom should be the rule, not the exception.

29

I owe oblivion nothing, and it has nothing to offer me except itself.

30

Each of us should have an island we can row to when the ship we're sailing loses course.

July

COWBOYS, One

Brave
they straddle the animals,
hearts racing before the pistol sings
then leaping from the chute
man and animal as one
wedded groin to back.

One small moment in the air
and then the mud.

Hats retrieved
Levis dusted
back to the bull pen
to await the next event.

Sunday's choirboys,
in cowboy hats.

COWBOYS, Two

Huddled in the pits
below the grandstand
or lining at the telephone
to call home victories
they make a gentle picture.
Their billfolds bulging just enough
to make another entrance fee.

Next week Omaha or Dallas.
San Antonio is yet to come.
And now the Cheyenne autumn
like a golden thread
ties them till the weekend's done.

COWBOYS, Three

They wade through beer cans
piled ankle high in gutters—
the rodeo has moved
    down from the fairground
to the town
and every hotel door's ajar.
Better than the Mardi Gras.
The nights are longer than Alaska now
until the main event begins
        another afternoon.

But after all the Main Event is still to be a cowboy.
For ten minutes or ten years, it's all the same.
You don't forget the Levis
        hugging you all day
and Stetson hats checked in passing windows
    cocked a certain way.

Some years later
when the bellies
flow over the belt loops
there're always mental photographs.
    Here the hero in mid-air.
Now the Dallas hotel room.
Now again the gaping tourists
licking off the Levis with their eyes.
Photographs of feeling
    mirrored in the mind.

from *Lonesome Cities*, 1968

July is the middle and both ends. A time to fiddle and make friends. 1

Loving is the only sure road out of darkness,
the only serum known to cure self-centeredness. 2

So much is passed off, praised and handed down
as love and loving in this life that reality at best
must be unreal. 3

4 My pledge of allegiance is a handshake. My anthem is my brother's shoulder. My flag is every smile that returns my own.

5 I am too busy trying to repay my share to offer an apology of any kind for a country that doesn't need one.

6 Had I invented love, I would have vaccinated the whole world.

There has been no time within our history
when patriots were not essential—
not one hundred years ago, not today, not tomorrow. 7

Don't place your heroes up too high.
They make an awful thunder when they all fall down. 8

We cannot be sustained by dreams alone. Strength is in the deed,
weakness in our unwillingness to perform it. 9

10

Let no one presume to write your history.
Live it.

11

All of us are falling, but we never realize it until we land.

12

When one becomes aware of achieving greatness . . .
their ability to be truly great is usually diminished.

Nobody's perfect, and that's one of the best things that can be said about man. 13

Being a lover doesn't necessarily make one capable of loving. 14

Loving and being loved have taken me down every road I ever wanted to travel, up every hill I felt the need to climb. 15

16 There is no wrong side or right side.
No misery in not being loved—only in not loving.

17 None of us is so wealthy or influential that
we cannot be further enriched by love.

18 What's right with our country is
those who go on righting wrongs.

What lies over the hill is probably one more hill.

19

The best way to climb a hill is to put one foot in front of the other and start up.

20

Hills have never worried me.
It's the valleys that are treacherous.

21

22

Only lonely men know freedom.
Love, as lovely as it is, still ensnares.

23

Welcome is the thunder
to the man who's lived too long in silence.

24

Conscience is a fragile thread. Whistle and it flies.

For years we've passed *it* off as boredom.
It's only now we recognize it by its real name: Peace.

25

Life is only little stops along the highway,
the railroad right-of-way, or our common corridors;
time the only punctuation.

26

Secrets flow like gossip in the night.
And, in the end, are just as unimportant.

27

28 Women want the near-impossible. Knowing that,
the wise man stays ready. We ask the difficult ourselves.
Love us. For ourselves.

29 The enemy of distance is delight.

30 It's always the strangers who do the most damage,
the ones you never get to know.

31

Why does it take so long to learn life's most important lesson: how to look at things in more than just a single way?

August

BUFFALO GRASS

Come, we'll all plant buffalo grass
and wade down ditches to the river
and each of us will take a lover,
someone new who'll never ask
why our eyes are puffed and red,
why our hopes of love are dead,
why we each go home to bed,
alone though we're together,
but never letting on
just growing older in the dawn
till the harvest finds us
no longer equal to the task
and cuts us down like so much buffalo grass.

from *Listen to the Warm*, 1967

The day's so warm, you wouldn't dare touch it 1
if it lay down by your side.

Eyes that look on love are easily the windows of the world. 2

When being judged, never ask "compared to what?" 3
You might receive an answer.

4

We may be lifted high by love, but to stay there
we must continue to care for what we left below,
remembering that it is not only possible but *necessary*
to share . . . everything.

5

Perhaps for all of us some penal purgatory is necessary
to purify the soul from the passions and pollutions
by which it has been stained in its connection with the body.

6

In becoming part of someone else you lose yourself,
and that's the very least that happens.

In the name of being and all human beings, I ask that you begin to *be* as soon as you begin to *see*. Merely seeing is not quite enough. 7

Sometimes seeing sunshine only takes looking in a mirror over someone else's shoulder. 8

If age has not made me a man agreeable, still I'm less demanding. 9

10

Rest assured that you will never rest assured. Not in this world.

11

I am only one more man trying all the best ways I know to make it through one more day.

12

To lie a little is not so bad if it gets you through the night.

If you've quarreled, make it right before the sun sets. **13**

What we want we cannot have.
What we have we've long ago stopped wanting. **14**

For a church to be a place of God,
it ought to be visited by God-like people. **15**

---

16 I know now space and time are coming. Enough to give me all the hours the new math needs for adding, multiplying, and dividing emptiness and dust and ceiling cracks.

---

17 Straight lines are sometimes difficult to walk and good for little more than proof of our sobriety on public highways.

---

18 Tomorrow is only tomorrow. There is nothing to fear except the coming of another day.

Disguises are so named because they are temporary.
Even the chameleon cannot slough off its skin. **19**

Not every wound the wounded carry leaves a visible scar. **20**

Only by working can we work. Only by practice is life lived.
Only by loving do we become fit to love. **21**

22 In love or out of love, we are suspended as in a limbo created by the presence of or the lack of someone else.

---

23 Your body lying easy in the August day is not
a challenge but an invitation. Being lazy too,
I leave it to the sun to ravage.

---

24 We come into the world alone and go away the same.
We're meant to spend the interval in closeness,
but it's a long while between the morning and the evening.

Understanding friends are few. Many who pretend friendship lack a certain sadness that betrays the truth.

25

Life is made easier by the joining of hands.

26

You will not meet another man more impatient
or closer to the starting gate than me. I hurry because
the clock's two hands are ahead of me.

27

28 A phrase of love can be strung out in such a way
that hate, by contrast, sounds more beautiful.

---

29 A woman speaking gently (or with strength) can tilt the world,
make it turn and twist and twirl across and off its axis.

---

30 It is man's nature to belittle women. What a pity,
what a heaped-up, heavy loss that could be done away with
to our mutual advantage.

31

The sea gets hungry every August, tired of eating only rivers.
So when the glances end on shore,
take your ankles to the water.

ADDED ATTRACTION

Sundays. Here are a month of them to play with.

On Sunday I stay in bed. Open all the windows. Work in the garden. Tear up all the junk mail. Stretch. Clean the house or rearrange the stacks of things I plan to go through one day. Take a bicycle ride. Drive to the beach. Send postcards. Run up the phone bill. Listen to Mozart, Morricone, Paul Simon, The Police, Bob Marley, Bach—if I'm up, Brahms; if I'm down, Borodin, Sinatra, Ella, and Sylvia Syms. Groom the cats and dogs. Stay in bed. Edit video tapes. Write. Ignore deadlines—mine and everybody else's. Read Walt Whitman, Emily Dickinson, Robert Bly, Nikki Giovanni, Joan Didion, Charles Plymell, Charles Bukowski, Aram Saroyan, Elaine Goodman, and new books friends have written. Make yet another list of things to do (that won't be done). Go ballooning. Paint. Draw Nicki or Bingo if they're sleeping. (Cats are hard to draw.) Wash the car. Rewrite my will. Stay in bed. Call up the White House, just for fun. (The number is 202 456-1414.) Daydream. Make popcorn or bloody marys. Cancel charge accounts. Read old magazines and last week's newspapers. Stay in bed. Overdub bad or incomplete vocals. Watch reruns of Carol Burnett. Swim. Catch up on the Bills (Safire and Buckley). Give liberal writers equal time. Pray. Make love, if I'm lucky.

On Sunday I don't usually go out to dinner. Sing in the shower. Answer the telephone. Answer the door. Read my own books. Exercise. Make my bed. Think about income tax. Go dancing. Weigh myself. Do crossword puzzles. Play bridge, Scrabble, darts, backgammon. Listen to new wave music. Argue. Comb my hair. Write my congressional representatives.

A Month of
Sundays
PRESTON

Sundays

I ROLL BETTER WITH THE NIGHT

Wrestling with the morning
I come out the loser
lying on the mat
looking up between the thighs of today.
I imagine myself
being picked up
        held, not let go.
Friendly hands
slipped into my back pockets
holding me close against new shoulders
then across my back
hands becoming arms
keep on holding me.

I roll better with the night.
I come up easy in the night
falling back
only when I'm tired and happy.

I don't mean to be indelicate
but I am always amazed
on meeting someone,

later mouthing them all over
all night long,
then in the morning they leave
afraid to use my toothbrush.

My mouth's been in and out of yours
and in and out of you so much
that scrubbing down with your toothbrush
is like eating cool mint jelly beans.

It's seven A.M.
another twenty minutes
and we'll both be late.
I don't want to move
and, anyway, my arm's asleep.

I know, I know.
Go, if you like,
but brush your teeth first
on the way to work
you might meet someone
you'd like to smell especially sweet for.

from *Celebrations of the Heart*, 1975

1 Sunday is for sleeping, sharing, staring, caring for all your ills.
For praying, playing, staying home, and paying bills.

2 You owe it to yourself to owe yourself nothing.

3 Saturday night is better than Friday. If you don't make out, you can take home the great American consolation prize, the Sunday paper.

I defy a headache or stomach grumble to order me away from hope. **4**

We have a special name for people who agree with us, **5**
we call them geniuses.

There's not much fuzz on an apple **6**
and very little hair on a grape.
It's only the lack of a beard on a peach
that keeps it from being an ape.

7

If you hear the music, join the singing.

8

The problem with alcohol is
not enough people stuff cotton in their mouths
when they use it.

9

The poor folks live on gravy. The rich folks live on steak.
The rich folks all have swimming pools
but they all go swimming in the lake.

Bend the rule too often and you might have to scrap the plan. **10**

What this country needs is a good twenty-five-cent quarter. **11**

Just wait until we get the bill for the indiscretions we've committed in the last dozen decades or so. **12**

13 Saturday keeps secrets that Sunday never could.

14 The battle to remain myself has been easy.
I took it to the streets.

15 If you believe in nothing, expect nothing as a reward.

It isn't necessary to believe in miracles.
Just hope a few believe in you.

16

Ballroom dancers should be stopped
whenever they attempt *Swan Lake.*

17

If you really want something, ask for it.
The most confusing thing anyone can say to you is *yes.*

18

19

Argue only with your peers,
otherwise there is no basis for an argument.

20

Nothing in the world is so bad
as something we call "not so bad."

21

It is a fact and not a pun that some heft and hoist barbells to attract bar belles. Some work out to keep from going out and working.

Anarchy is anarchy only from the standpoint of other people's concepts of order. 22

While the fast lane gets you there the soonest,
the outside lane cannot be ignored. 23

Pray for me. My sins are many, some unforgivable.
Your help would be appreciated. 24

---

25 Simple men sometimes conceal genius in their ears and pockets, a rabbit in the hat, scarves with dazzling colors appear and disappear from nowhere, bright balloons from Brigadoon, pigeons, doves, and other birds come from ears and noses. In other words, not only birds, but who in life turns out to be
what anyone supposes?

---

26 Being born a bastard gave me an advantage over all those people who spend their entire lives becoming one.

---

27 God is wise beyond all years and decades He sent
driving through the rain, and so I have my father's ears
and, on good days, my mother's brain.

Why quit while you're losing? 28

Leave your mark on something, preferably very gently. 29

I will go down death's road by myself and hope
to leave behind but one memorial: a lifeless body
that did not acquaint itself with compromise. 30

31

A book is never finished.
It's only stopped and sent off to the printer.

ABOUT THE AUTHOR

Rod McKuen has traveled throughout the world pursuing more than a dozen occupations, although he is best known as a poet, composer, columnist, lecturer, and performer. As recipient of the Carl Sandburg Award, he was acclaimed "the people's poet—because he has made poetry a part of so many people's lives." With poetry that is able to touch directly the heart of the reader, it is little wonder that McKuen's books have sold in excess of 30 million copies and that his work is taught and studied in schools, colleges, universities, and seminaries throughout the world.

Among the many awards Mr. McKuen has received are the Freedom Foundation Medal of Honor, The First Amendment Society Man of the Year Award, the University of Detroit Humanitarian Award, the Horatio Alger Award, and the Man of the Year Citation from the Menninger Foundation. He has won the Grande Prix du Disc (France's most prestigious award for recordings) an unprecedented seven times, and is the recipient of several Grammy and Golden Globe awards.

With over 2,000 songs (accounting for sales of over 200 million records) to his credit, McKuen is one of the most prolific composer/lyricists writing today. His music ranges from gold-record popular standards (such as "Jean," "If You Go Away," "Love's Been Good to Me," "Seasons in the Sun," "The World I Used to Know," and "I'll Catch the Sun") to widely performed classical compositions that have joined the standard repertoire of leading symphony, choral, and chamber groups internationally. His suite for orchestra and narrator, entitled *The City,* a commissioned work for the Louisville Orchestra, was nominated for the Pulitzer Prize in music. Other major McKuen classical compositions have been premiered at Carnegie Hall, London's Royal Albert Hall, the Hollywood Bowl, the Concertgebouw in Amsterdam, and the Brahmsaal in Vienna.

The Black Eagle, McKuen's new "gothic musical" of operatic scope, incorporates dance, solo and ensemble choral work, and film effects. Already a best-selling album, the show is being presented in various cities around the world.

In his travels of the past decade, Rod McKuen has given over 2,000 concerts and lectures in twenty-five countries. His film scores for over a dozen motion pictures include *The Prime of Miss Jean Brodie, Joanna, A Boy Named Charlie Brown, Lisa Bright and Dark, Disney's Scandalous John, The Borrowers,* and *The Unknown War,* twenty hours of documentary film co-produced by Russian and American film companies.

Future travels will take him to China, the Middle East, Australia, throughout Europe, and behind the Iron Curtain for new writing and performing projects. Included will be several major commissions for classical music, a children's book, television specials, the creation of ballet scores for the American Dance Ensemble, which premieres a series of McKuen ballets every year, and several unique recording projects.

After completing three books this year, the author took his first vacation in several years—almost three months, "somewhere."